TRADE  MARK

THE SINGLETON

WHISKEY

Single Malt Scotch Whisky

PRODUCT
OF SCOTLAND

of Dufftown

TRADITIONALLY DISTILLED

MATURED FOR **12** TWELVE YEARS

PaRRagon

Bath • New York • Cologne • Melbourne • Delhi
Hong Kong • Shenzhen • Singapore • Amsterdam

This edition published by Parragon
Books Ltd in 2015 and distributed by

Parragon Inc.
440 Park Avenue South, 13th Floor
New York, NY 10016
www.parragon.com

ISBN 978-1-4748-0669-5
Printed in China

Contents

Introduction

Despite the huge variety of "types" available around the world, true whiskey is always made from three simple ingredients: Water, grain and yeast. It is the distiller's alchemy that transforms these ingredients into "whiskey," which in Gaelic means "water of life."

The importance of water quality should not be underestimated; locations for distilleries have traditionally been selected according to the proximity of a good water source.

Each whiskey consists of one or several types of grain, usually barley, corn, or rye, the quality and combination of which has a major effect on the character of the final product. The distilleries that use a variety of grains each have their own unique and often top secret recipe.

Until as recently as the 19th century the process of fermentation was not fully understood: Yeast, the micro-organism that converts sugar into alcohol, is naturally present in the air, and successful fermentation was a rather hit-and-miss affair. The monks who traditionally brewed alcohol in the West considered the transformation to be "God's gift." It was the scientist Louis Pasteur who discovered that yeasts could be cultured and the fermentation process controlled. Yeast can also add a certain "fruitiness" to the flavor of the whiskey.

The process of making whiskey is deceptively simple. First, the grain is "mashed" with water, which breaks down starch in the grain into sugars to create a malty liquid called "wort." The wort is fermented by the addition of yeast. If this sounds very much like the production of beer, that's more or less what it is at this stage. However, the beer—or "wash," as it is known in Scotland—is just the ore from which the "liquid gold" is extracted by the process of distillation. Distillation traditionally takes place in copper stills, in which the beer is heated to release the spirit.

So, is this "liquid gold" the wonderful golden color that we associate with fine whiskeys? Well, no, at this stage it is crystal clear. Whiskey has to mature in a cask (usually oak) and it is the length of maturation that imparts color to the whiskey and further enhances its character. The location in which the barrels are stored is also important; depending on the local climate, maturation times can vary widely.

To complicate matters, much of the whiskey on sale is a blend of a variety of whiskeys mixed in a specific quantity of "single malt" (made exclusively from malted barley) and "grain whiskey" (usually made with at least 51 percent corn) to give a consistent character to the end product.

So where do you begin to explore this wonderful but bewildering world of whiskey? Well, the good news is that you have made a great start by buying this book with the handy whiskey flask. The tasting notes will help you find a place to begin your journey but ultimately it will be your own taste buds that guide you to your favorite whiskeys. And wherever your taste buds lead you, the joy is definitely in the journey itself. Good whiskey hunting and good health!

SCOTLAND

There are more distilleries in this small but magical country than in the rest of the world combined—a testament to the Scots' passion for their national beverage.

Scotland is a great place to begin a journey into the world of whiskey. To legally be called "scotch," the whisky (always spelt without an "e") has to be wholly matured in Scotland in oak casks for a period of at least three years. Although other grains can be included in Scottish whiskies, "malt whisky" must be made entirely from malted barley. Scotland is famous for its "single malts" where all the malt whisky is produced at the same distillery. If whiskies of different ages are blended, only the youngest may be stated on the label.

Ardmore

Founded in 1898, the Ardmore Distillery was built to provide a core single-malt whisky for Teacher's Highland Cream. The distillery is fed by springs from Knockandy Hill and all Ardmore whiskies use aromatic smoke from highland-peat fires to dry the barley. Fermentation takes place in vessels crafted from Oregon pine rather than steel and Ardmore employs a double-maturation process—with an initial maturation in traditional American-oak bourbon casks followed by a second maturation in small 19th-century quarter casks.

Tasting Notes

Sweet malt leads the way on the nose, followed by an earthy peatiness. The taste is complex with a burst of sweet, creamy vanilla and malt flavors followed by emerging notes of heather and honey. The finish is long and smooth.

Ardmore Highland Single Malt.
46% ABV.
Color: Pale bronze.

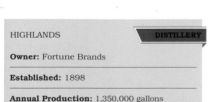

HIGHLANDS **DISTILLERY**

Owner: Fortune Brands

Established: 1898

Annual Production: 1,350,000 gallons

Balblair

Founded in 1790 by John Ross, the Balblair Distillery is located in a highly picturesque setting on the Dornoch Firth. It is the second-oldest distillery in Scotland. Nowadays, Balblair whiskies are uniquely vintage, named for the year they were made: The distillery manager selects the casks that best exemplify Balblair single malts, which are typically fruity and smooth. The American-oak, ex-bourbon casks used in maturation impart distinctive taffy and vanilla notes.

Tasting Notes

The nose of this 16-year-old whisky is very fresh and light. On the palate, it reveals a light note of peat, with a slightly sweet hint of citrus. The long finish is fresh, complex, and fruity.

Balblair Single Malt. Aged 16 years.
40% ABV. Color: Amber.

HIGHLANDS	DISTILLERY
Owner: Inver House	
Established: 1790	
Annual Production: 350,000 gallons	

Tasting Notes

The nose of this 12-year-old whisky has sweet fruit and sherry notes, layered with rich honey and vanilla. The sweet sherry note develops on the palate with elements of cinnamon. The finish is long and warming.

The Balvenie Double Wood, Single Malt.
Aged 12 years.
40% ABV.
Color: Dark amber.

DISTILLERY

SPEYSIDE

Owner: William Grant & Sons

Established: 1892

Annual Production: 1,480,000 gallons

Balvenie

Balvenie Distillery sits between Craigellachie and the "whisky capital," Dufftown. William Grant and his sons built the distillery in 1892 and it remains with the family to this day, together with its sister distilleries: Kininvie and Glenfiddich. Balvenie is one of the few remaining distilleries to have its own maltings floor, and it also grows a proportion of its own barley. It has nine stills that produce a single malt with a famously strong element of honey.

Tasting Notes

This is a wonderfully balanced whisky with notes of chocolate in the citrusy aroma, orange and coffee on the palate, and a pleasurable mandarin finish.

The Dalmore Single Malt.
Aged 15 years.
40% ABV.
Color: Orange amber.

Dalmore

Located on the northern shores of the Firth of Cromarty, in the Northern Highlands, Dalmore Distillery harnesses the waters of Loch Morie and the barley fields of the rich coastal soils of the Black Isle to produce exceptional single-malt whisky. The distillery was established in 1839 and the iconic stag's head from the Mackenzie family crest adorns every exquisitely packaged bottle of Dalmore single malt.

DISTILLERY

HIGHLANDS

Owner: United Breweries Group

Established: 1839

Annual Production: 1,110,000 gallons

Dalwhinnie

Established in 1897, the Dalwhinnie Distillery is the highest in Scotland, sited on the edge of the town of the same name. It is located on the railroad line between Glasgow and Fort William and within sight of the A9 highway. Its visitors' center is open throughout the year but is often snowed in, in winter, due to its high location. The distillery retains some interesting traditional equipment, including wooden worm tubs, to produce whisky that is full bodied, smooth, and warming.

DISTILLERY

SPEYSIDE

Owner: Diageo

Established: 1897

Annual Production: 360,000 gallons

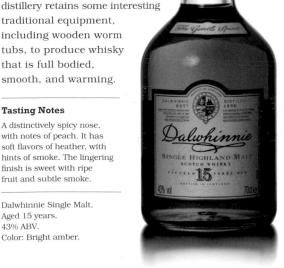

Tasting Notes

A distinctively spicy nose, with notes of peach. It has soft flavors of heather, with hints of smoke. The lingering finish is sweet with ripe fruit and subtle smoke.

Dalwhinnie Single Malt.
Aged 15 years.
43% ABV.
Color: Bright amber.

Tasting Notes

This smooth, naturally rich single-malt whisky has aromas of roasted nuts with sweet fruity notes; a classic Speyside fruity palate with hints of blackcurrant and coffee; and an initially dry, lingering, and pleasurably warm finish.

The Singleton Single Malt.
Aged 12 years.
43% ABV.
Color: Deep gold.

DISTILLERY

SPEYSIDE

Owner: Diageo

Established: 1896

Annual Production: 1,530,000 gallons

Dufftown

Distilled since 1896 with pure water from Highlandman John's Well, the new-make spirit that runs from the three pairs of stills is spicy in character and, as it says on the label, "perfectly balanced, naturally rich and smooth" following 12 years in a combination of American and European oak casks. The distinctive bottle shape suggests a traditional hip flask while the color of the glass is inspired by the blue flint glass used at the turn of the 20th century.

Glen Spey

Built by James Stuart in 1878, the Glen Spey Distillery stands on the main road in the center of Rothes, just north of Craigellachie in Speyside. The attractive Victorian weathered-stone distillery has four stills and mainly produces whisky for J&B blends. Much of the interior, too, is in period. The whisky is produced with water from the Doonie Burn and is characteristically light, grassy, and slightly peaty.

Tasting Notes

The nose is light, malty, and lightly spiced with notes of chocolate. The palate has some vanilla, honey, and lightly roasted nuts. The long finish is light and slightly dry with a wisp of smoke.

Glen Spey Single Malt (Flora & Fauna). Aged 12 years. 43% ABV. Color: Golden yellow.

SPEYSIDE	DISTILLERY

Owner: Diageo

Established: 1878

Annual Production: 370,000 gallons

Glenallachie

Set in pleasant meadowland southwest of Craigellachie in Speyside, Glenallachie is a relatively modern distillery that produces whisky for blends such as Clan Campbell. It was built in 1967 and has a stainless-steel mash tun, two beer stills, and two spirit stills. The distillery produces whisky with a delicate, subtle and light-yet-complex character that makes it an ideal aperitif. However, single-malt bottlings are relatively rare.

Tasting Notes

The nose is quite light with aromas of dry grass and notes of barley sugars and honey. The palate has notes of barley and taffy with a hint of charred oak. The medium-long finish has a spicy warmth.

Glenallachie Single Malt (Connoisseurs Choice), 1992. 43% ABV. Color: Straw yellow.

SPEYSIDE   DISTILLERY

Owner: Pernod Ricard

Established: 1967

Annual Production: 850,000 gallons

Glenfiddich

Located in the whisky capital of Dufftown in the beautiful Fiddich Valley, Glenfiddich, meaning "Valley of the Deer," is little changed since 1887, when William Grant and his nine children built the distillery themselves using money saved by William over a 20-year period. Today, still family-owned five generations on, Glenfiddich produces the world's favorite single-malt scotch whisky. The distillery boasts two stainless-steel mash tuns, 24 Douglas-fir washbacks, and 28 stills.

Tasting Notes

It has a smoky aroma stemming from a finishing period in casks previously used for a smoky malt, with notes of orange. The palate is very full and fruity, with a light note of peat. The finish is long and creamy, also with a hint of smoke.

DISTILLERY

SPEYSIDE

Owner: William Grant & Sons

Established: 1887

Annual Production: 2,640,000 gallons

Glenfiddich Single Malt. Aged 12 years. 40% ABV. Color: Golden.

Glenturret

Set on the outskirts of the village of Crieff in the Turret River Valley, Glenturret was established in 1775 and proudly claims to be Scotland's oldest distillery. Glenturret single malt is very complex, fresh, flowery, and dry, and is renowned for being an important part of the hugely popular Famous Grouse blend. The distillery was closed for a thirty-year period but was reopened in 1959 by James Fairlie and quickly returned to its former (and present) glory. It is a major tourist attraction drawing thousands of visitors every year.

Tasting Notes

The nose has a wonderfully sweet sherry note with a little smokiness and malt. The malt continues on the palate, with notes of sherry and pepper. The finish is medium-long and a little creamy.

The Glenturret Single Malt. Aged 10 Years.
40% ABV. Color: Pale amber.

CENTRAL LOWLANDS	DISTILLERY
Owner: The Edrington Group	
Established: 1775	
Annual Production: 90,000 gallons	

Johnnie Walker

Originally known as Walker's Kilmarnock Whisky, the world-famous blend has humble origins as John Walker sold whisky as part of his grocer's business in Ayrshire, Scotland. It was John's son Alexander and grandson Alexander II who started marketing the whisky in earnest, introducing the iconic square bottle and the slanted label. In 2009, Diageo controversially shifted production from Kilmarnock to Leven, Fife.

DISTILLERY

KILMARNOCK

Owner: Diageo

Established: ca.1870

Status: Closed

Johnnie Walker Black Label. Blended. Aged 12 years. 40% ABV. Color: Rich amber.

Tasting Notes

Comprising some 40 different malts and grains, it has complex aromas with citrus and a hint of peat, and sweet notes of malt and honey. It is bold on the palate, with fruit, vanilla, and well-balanced grains. The finish is long and spicy, with sherry and a delicate wisp of smoke.

Tasting Notes

The nose has a slight aroma of peat, with notes of honey and marzipan. The peat and honey are present on the palate, with a distinct spicy note. The finish is pleasantly sweet.

Isle of Jura Single Malt.
Aged 10 years.
45% ABV.
Color: Amber.

Jura

The distillery was established in 1810 by Laird Archibald Campbell, although distilling is known to have been carried out illegally on the island of Jura since the 17th century. Using water from Loch a Bhaille Mhargaidh, the whisky is characteristically light and salty with a trace of peat. Often called "the Highland from the Island," it is said to have more in common with Highland whisky than with that from neighboring Islay.

DISTILLERY

ISLE OF JURA

Owner: United Spirits Group

Established: 1810

Annual Production: 580,000 gallons

Lagavulin

The ruins of Dunyvaig Castle, once home to the Lords of Islay of the MacDonald clan, lie within view of the Lagavulin Distillery on the Hebridean island of Islay. The distillery was established in the early 19th century and until recently produced malt exclusively for the famous White Horse blend. Since Diageo began marketing Lagavulin as one of its six Classic Malts of Scotland, production has struggled to keep up with demand.

Tasting Notes

The nose is very complex: smoky, peaty, and sophisticated, with notes of sherry. The aroma is echoed on the palate but with additional notes of salt and hay. The finish is long and peaty.

Lagavulin Single Malt. Aged 16 years. 43% ABV. Color: Deep amber.

ISLAY	DISTILLERY
Owner: Diageo	
Established: ca.1815	
Annual Production: 590,000 gallons	

Laphroaig

Laphroaig Distillery sits in a picturesque bay on the coast of Islay. It was established in the early 19th century and is one of the very few distilleries that still uses traditional malting floors. Legend has it that its original owner Donald Johnston drowned in a vat of his own whisky in 1847. Today, Laphroaig is famous for its "marmite effect," you either love it or you hate it. It has a strong, almost medicinal flavor that those who fall into the "hate" camp compare to mouthwash!

Tasting Notes

This cask-strength single malt has a pronounced phenolic nose and medium body. The flavor is medicinal with notes of salt and seaweed. The finish, too, is medicinal and peaty with notes of tar.

Laphroaig Single Malt, Aged 10 years. 57.3% ABV.
Color: Pale golden yellow.

ISLAY	DISTILLERY
Owner: Fortune Brands	
Established: ca.1815	
Annual Production: 710,000 gallons	

Loch Lomond

Loch Lomond Distillery is situated in Alexandria on the Leven River, south of the loch that gives the whisky its name. It has its own cooperage, 18 washbacks, three sets of malt stills, and a column still for grain whisky. Consequently, production is varied with several different types of whisky being made at this facility.

Loch Lomond Single
Malt. Aged 21 years.
40% ABV.
Color: Golden.

Tasting Notes

The 21-year-old has a delicate floral aroma. The long oak-cask maturation shows in the flavor, with notes of malt and honey. The finish is lingering with a whiff of smoke.

DISTILLERY

HIGHLANDS

Owner: Loch Lomond Distillers

Established: 1965

Annual Production: 3,170,000 gallons

Mortlach

Located on the outskirts of Dufftown, near to Mortlach Kirk (one of the oldest churches in Scotland), the distillery was founded in the early 19th century and its whisky has always been very popular with blenders—most notably for Johnnie Walker. The distillery layout is unusual in that the stills are of different sizes and are not paired off—in 1897 capacity was doubled when three additional stills were added to the original three.

Tasting Notes

The aroma is lightly smoky with notes of orange. The flavor is pleasantly nutty with just the faintest hint of salt. In the finish, the nutty influences are accompanied by a return of the light smoke.

Mortlach Single Malt. Aged 16 years. 43% ABV. Color: Rich mahogany.

SPEYSIDE	DISTILLERY
Owner: Diageo	
Established: 1823	
Annual Production: 770,000 gallons	

Oban

Oban Distillery was founded by the Stevenson brothers, John and Hugh, in 1793. The enterprising brothers also established a tannery and a boat-building yard in the area, and the success of their ventures led to the growth of the coastal town of Oban. The Oban Distillery has only two stills and cannot expand due to space restrictions in the small town that surrounds it. This limitation also affects storage: The casks cannot mature exclusively in the adjacent warehouses.

DISTILLERY

HIGHLANDS

Owner: Diageo

Established: 1793

Annual Production: 180,000 gallons

Oban Single Malt. Aged 14 years.
43% ABV.
Color: Deep straw gold.

Tasting Notes

This is a slightly smoky yet fruity and sweet whisky with a nose of toasted malt. The flavor is malty with notes of spice. The finish is mild yet remarkably long and dry with just a hint of salt.

Pittyvaich

Arhur Bell & Sons founded the Pittyvaich Distillery in 1975 to produce whisky for blends. It was the eighth distillery to be built in Dufftown, making obselete the local axiom: "Rome was built on seven hills, Dufftown was built on seven stills." More recently, the distillery was bought by Diageo and used to experiment with different types of barley and novel distilling techniques. In 2002, Pittyvaich was closed for good and demolished.

DISTILLERY

SPEYSIDE

Owner: Diageo

Established: 1975

Status: Demolished

Pittyvaich Single Malt
(Flora & Fauna).
Aged 12 years.
43% ABV.
Color: Deep straw gold.

Tasting Notes

The nose is very clean and fruity with a fine, strong note of sherry. The flavor is vibrant and fruity with a little malt. The finish is long, dry, and aromatic.

Royal Lochnagar

John Begg founded the distillery in 1845 and struggled initially due to conflict with illegal distilleries. However, his fortunes changed for the better following the arrival of a new neighbor at nearby Balmoral Castle. Queen Victoria was enthusiastic about everything to do with the Highlands and accepted an invitation to visit the distillery with her family. Her Majesty *was* amused, and Lochnagar was named as an official supplier to the Crown.

Tasting Notes

The aroma is full with a sour-fruit character. The fruity flavors develop on the palate into a malty sweetness, with the faint suggestion of smoke. The finish is soft and long.

Royal Lochnagar Single Malt. Aged 12 years. 43% ABV. Color: Pale amber.

HIGHLANDS	DISTILLERY

Owner: Diageo

Established: 1845

Annual Production: 120,000 gallons

Scapa

SCOTLAND

Located on Mainland in the Orkney Islands, close to the historic Scapa Flow, the distillery was founded by Macfarlane and Townsend. It has a Lomond pattern beer still and a conventional spirit still, and its whisky is matured in American oak bourbon casks in traditional dunnage warehouses producing whisky that is characteristically salty and oily with notes of seaweed, chocolate, and heather. It is used in the production of blends as well as for some official single malts.

Tasting Notes

The nose is sweet with notes of honey and orange. The palate is full-bodied with notes of heather and grasses, and a hint of oak and cinnamon. The finish is long with notes of oak and a wisp of smoke.

Scapa Single Malt, Aged 16 years. 40% ABV.
Color: Pale amber.

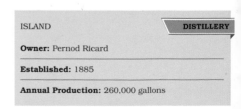

ISLAND

DISTILLERY

Owner: Pernod Ricard

Established: 1885

Annual Production: 260,000 gallons

Speyburn

Located in a lovely valley near Rothes in Speyside, Speyburn is renowned for being "the most photographed distillery in Scotland." It dates back to 1897, the year in which Queen Victoria celebrated her 60th jubilee. Relatively little has changed since then. There is a traditional rake mash tun feeding wort into six Oregon-pine washbacks. The still room has just a single pair of stills. The soft spring water from the Granty Burn is said to give this whisky its distinctive floral character.

DISTILLERY

SPEYSIDE

Owner: AB InBev

Established: 1897

Annual Production: 530,000 gallons

Speyburn Single Malt. Aged 10 years. 40% ABV. Color: Pale gold.

Tasting Notes

The nose is sweet with citrus notes and a hint of hay. It is medium-bodied with a delicate fruity character and notes of heather. The finish is warm and malty.

Tasting Notes

The nose is very sweet with notes of orange and oak and the slightest hint of smoke. It is medium-bodied with a fruity flavor and notes of sherry. The finish is long and exceptionally complex with strong smoky and spicy notes.

Springbank 100 Proof Single Malt. Aged 10 years.
57% ABV.
Color: Straw gold.

DISTILLERY

CAMPBELTOWN

Owner: J&A Mitchell

Established: 1828

Annual Production: 530,000 gallons

Springbank

The distillery is located in the city of Campbeltown in the south of the Kintyre Peninsula. Established by the Mitchell family, who still own it to this day, it is the only distillery left in Scotland that carries out all the whisky-production processes in-house, including the use of its own bottling plant. It is also the only distillery in Scotland to produce three styles of single malt—Springbank, Longrow, and Hazelburn—achieved by the use of three different production methods.

Talisker

The Talisker Distillery stands in a very picturesque spot on the shores of Loch Harport on the Isle of Skye, fed by the intensely peaty waters of the Cnoc Nan Speireag spring. Dating from 1831, the distillery was extended in 1900 and triple distillation was practiced until 1928, which explains the unusual layout of five stills. This is a highly complex and unconventional whisky with a distinct peppery flavor that adds to its warming spiciness.

Talisker Single Malt.
Aged 10 years.
45.8% ABV.
Color: Golden yellow.

Tasting Notes

The nose has a characteristic peatiness with notes of seawater and a slight citrusy sweetness. It is full-bodied with a fruity sweetness and smoke and malt flavors, with a strong note of pepper at back of the palate. It has a long and intense peppery finish.

DISTILLERY

ISLAND

Owner: Diageo

Established: 1831

Annual Production: 530,000 gallons

The Glenlivet

In the valley of the Livet River in Speyside stands The Glenlivet Distillery, near to the point where the Livet and Avon converge. It is the only distillery with official license to add "the" to its name to distinguish itself from all the other distilleries in the Livet Valley. It was founded by George Smith in 1824 but moved to its present location in 1858. The whisky has characteristics that many associate with the Livet River itself: Clarity, floweriness, and elegance.

Tasting Notes

The nose is sweet and floral with notes of vanilla and hints of aniseed, malt, and oak. The palate is quite fruity and warm, with echoes of aniseed and dry fruits. The finish is long and warming.

The Glenlivet Single Malt. Aged 12 years. 40% ABV. Color: Pale gold.

SPEYSIDE	DISTILLERY
Owner: Pernod Ricard	
Established: 1824	
Annual Production: 2,770,000 gallons	

Tasting Notes

The nose is light and citrusy with a hint of pear drops. It is somewhat oily and earthy on the palate, with notes of vanilla and a mild nuttiness. The medium finish is mildly woody with notes of spice.

Tullibardine Single Malt (Aged Oak Edition).
40% ABV.
Color: Pale gold.

Tullibardine

Located in Blackford, close to the renowned Gleneagles Hotel and golf courses, Tullibardine is fed from a spring in the Ochil Hills—the same spring that once served the ancient brewery that stood on the site and supplied beer to King James 1V as early as 1488. The brewery was converted into a distillery by William Delmé-Evans. Although mothballed in 1995, the distillery was given a new lease of life by a consortium of whisky connoisseurs in 2003.

DISTILLERY
HIGHLANDS
Owner: Picard Vins & Spiritueux
Established: 1949
Annual Production: 710,000 gallons

IRELAND

Although Ireland currently has far fewer distilleries than its neighbor across the Irish Sea, it nevertheless has a venerable history of whiskey production that goes back at least as far as that of Scotland.

Like Scottish whisky, Irish whiskey (which is always spelt with an "e") must be matured in wood for at least three years. Ireland is especially renowned for 'pure-pot-still' blends of malted and unmalted barley that are distilled three times as opposed to the twice-distilled whiskies of Scotland. Grains other than barley can be used to make Irish whiskey.

Single G

IRISH WHI

Bushmills

The world's oldest licensed distillery was established in the Bushmills area of County Antrim, Northern Ireland — a fact that is celebrated on the Bushmills label. From 1987 it belonged to Pernod Ricard but was transferred to Diageo in 2006 in order to fulfill the requirements of the Irish monopolies commission. Freshwater is supplied by St. Columb's Rill, a local stream that runs into the Bush River. A triple-distilled whiskey, Bushmills Malt is available in three bottlings: Aged 10, 16, and 21 years.

Tasting Notes

The nose is robust with notes of treacle and spice. It is full bodied with praline and honey on the palate, with a hint of chocolate. The finish is fruity and echoes the chocolate note on the palate.

COUNTY ANTRIM	DISTILLERY
Owner: Diageo	
Established: 1608	
Annual Production: 1,190,000 gallons	

Bushmills Single Malt,
Aged 16 years. 40% ABV.
Color: Amber.

Tasting Notes

The aroma is clean with light corn and notes of oak and honey. The taste is smooth and mellow with echoes of honey and a hint of almonds. There is some honey in the warm, dry finish.

Greenore Single Grain.
Aged 8 years.
40% ABV.
Color: Rich amber.

DISTILLERY

COUNTY LOUGH

Owner: Beam Inc.

Established: 1987

Annual Production: 1,320,000 gallons

Greenore

The Cooley Distillery is located in Riverstown just south of Dundalk and the border with Northern Ireland. It was founded in 1987 by John Teeling, who bought the Cimicei Distillery and renamed it Cooley after the nearby mountain range. Greenore is a single-grain whiskey made using high-quality corn and soft water from the Cooley Mountains. It is matured for eight years in bourbon oak casks in the distillery's Riverstown warehouse.

Jameson

Today, only a museum remains as a reminder of the famous Jameson Distillery that once stood in Bow Street, Dublin. It was founded in 1780 by the Scot John Jameson, whose family was known to strive for the highest quality. Noticing that a particular strain of barley was better for whiskey production, the Jamesons persuaded local farmers to grow the grain. The distillery was also among the first to appreciate the importance of maturation and pioneered the use of sherry barrels in the aging process.

Tasting Notes

The aroma is characterized by sherry notes and vanilla. On the palate, there is a strong, full-bodied, and sweet sherry flavor, with notes of dried fruits. Sherry once again comes to the fore in the pleasantly long finish.

DISTILLERY

DUBLIN

Owner: Pernod Ricard

Established: 1780

Status: Closed

Jameson. Aged 12 years, Blended. 40% ABV.
Color: Golden yellow.

Kilbeggan

Kilbeggan Distillery lies in the town of the same name in County Westmeath, west of Dublin. Whiskey was produced here from 1757 using a single still, and it was only in the late 19th century, when John Locke and his family bought and extended the facility, that whiskey was produced in earnest. Sadly, the family was forced to sell the distillery after World War II. Production ceased in 1953, and the distillery buildings were converted into a museum.

DISTILLERY

CO. WESTMEATH

Owner: Beam Inc.

Established: 1987

Annual Production: 1,320,000 gallons

Kilbeggan. Blended.
40% ABV.
Color: Pale gold.

Tasting Notes

Lemony scents immediately rise to the nose. On the palate, the citrus notes in the sweet flavor are joined by a light note of roasted malt. The finish is well balanced and dry.

Midleton Very Rare

Lying in the small southern town of Midleton, 15 miles from Cork, the distillery was founded by the Murphy brothers. Following massive expansion in the 1970s, production has to stay high to make it worthwhile operating the stills, but the distillery has the advantage of being incredibly flexible: The heart of the distillery consists of four pot stills and six column stills in a highly complex plant suitable for the production of a vast array of whiskeys.

Tasting Notes

The nose reveals a pronounced citrus note augmented by caramel. The palate echoes the nose, adding a slightly sweet malt flavor with a hint of spice. There is a medium-long, fruity finish.

Midleton Very Rare, 1990. Blended. 40% ABV. Color: Golden yellow.

COUNTY CORK	DISTILLERY

Owner: Pernod Ricard

Established: 1825

Annual Production: 5,280,000 gallons

Tasting Notes

The nose contains complex aromas of dried fruit with banana and apple, and notes of vanilla and almonds. The palate offers sherry and further fruits, such as pears and apricots. The finish is exceptionally long, with renewed sherry and raw barley.

Redbreast, Pure Pot Still.
Aged 12 years.
40% ABV.
Color: Bright bronze.

DISTILLERY

DUBLIN

Owner: Pernod Ricard

Established: 1780

Status: Closed

Redbreast

Redbreast first appeared on the market in 1939. It was produced by Jameson, but the Gilbey Company aged it in their own sherry casks, then bottled and marketed the resulting product. It already enjoyed an excellent reputation at the time. After the Jameson Distillery closed its gates, Gilbey continued to deliver Redbreast until the mid-1980s. Some connoisseurs consider this pure-pot-still whiskey to be one of the best that Ireland has to offer.

Tullamore Dew

The distillery was founded by Michael Molloy but it was the later owner Daniel E. Williams who added his initials to the Tullamore brand and used the catchy advertising slogan, "Give every man his Dew." Success was immediate, and Tullamore Dew became Ireland's best-known whiskey. The triple whammy of American prohibition, a trade war with England, and World War II led to the downfall of Tullamore along with so many other distilleries.

Tullamore Dew. Blended. Aged 12 years. 40% ABV. Color: Pale golden yellow.

Tasting Notes

This whiskey has a complex aroma, as do most blends with an unmistakable pot-still character. A sweet sherry note becomes apparent on the palate. Its astonishingly long finish has a slightly spicy effect.

DISTILLERY

COUNTY OFFALY

Owner: BC Partners

Established: 1829

Status: Closed

UNITED STATES OF AMERICA

Especially renowned for its many fabulous bourbons and charcoal-mellowed Tennessee whiskies, the USA is one of the great whiskey-producing nations. In the States, 'whiskey' is almost always spelt with an "e."

Bourbon has to contain at least 51 percent corn. Similarly, rye, malt, and wheat whiskies must all contain at least 51 percent of their respective grains. Most whiskies have to be aged in charred new oak casks, although no aging period is specified. To be labeled "straight," whiskey must be aged two years or more.

Buffalo Trace

The first modern distillery was built on this site in Buffalo Trace, east of Louisville, Kentucky, by gold prospector Benjamin Blanton. Today, there are two distilleries on the site and the total area, including storage, comprises some 110 buildings on 667 acres. In addition to Buffalo Trace Kentucky Straight Bourbon, the distillery creates numerous other finely crafted, award-winning spirits, including Blanton's, Old Charter, and Eagle Rare.

DISTILLERY

KENTUCKY

Owner: Sazerac

Established: 1857

Annual Production: Not specified

Buffalo Trace Kentucky Straight Bourbon. 40% ABV. Color: Light bronze.

Tasting Notes

The aroma is fruity-flowery with a light touch of wood and chocolate. Its flavors are complex and powerful, with corn and rye and notes of chocolate, leather, and cloves. The finish is long with notes of oak and a vanilla aftertaste.

Dickel

The George A. Dickel Distillery is found near Tullahoma, Tennessee. George Dickel discovered that whisky made in winter was smoother than that made in summer. To achieve this smoothness consistently he chilled the whisky before it was sent into the charcoal-mellowing vats. George declared that his whisky was as smooth as the finest scotch and labeled his "whisky" without an "e," in keeping with the Scottish tradition.

Tasting Notes

The nose is spicy but notably mild, with notes of fruit and rye. The medium-heavy palate is spicy and complex, with notes of cinnamon and ginger. The finish is very clean with a hint of apple pie.

George Dickel No.12.
45% ABV. Color: Reddish amber.

TENNESSEE	DISTILLERY
Owner: Dickel	
Established: 1870	
Annual Production: 1,190,000 gallons	

Tasting Notes

Today, there are three varieties of Four Roses. The Single Barrel Whiskey has a well-defined aroma of malt and vanilla. On the palate, rye comes through the spicy and complex flavor. The finish is sweetish, with a strong note of oak.

Four Roses Single Barrel. 43% ABV. Color: Pale reddish amber.

Four Roses

Whiskey dealer Paul Jones Jr. created the brand in honor of his wife who had worn a corsage of four red roses on the day she accepted his proposal of marriage. The whiskey itself is the result of a process marrying two different mash recipes, with five different yeasts, producing ten different beers, which are fermented in a variety of vats to be blended for the first time, only after the distillation process is complete.

DISTILLERY

KENTUCKY

Owner: Kirin

Established: 1860

Annual Production: 2,910,000 gallons

Heaven Hill

UNITED STATES

In the years immediately following prohibition, the Shapira brothers set up a business designed to permit the production of whiskey on a grand scale, and succeeded spectacularly. Heaven Hill has one of the largest whiskey inventories in the world, with more than 600,000 barrels. And this is despite a massive setback in 1996 when a lightning strike caused a fire that destroyed the still house and nine warehouses. In 1999, the company bought Bernheim Distillery from Diageo, giving Heaven Hill its own manufacturing base once more.

Tasting Notes

A no-frills Bourbon with a spicy nose. The taste is well balanced with notes of banana, cinnamon, and nutmeg. The medium finish is clean and spicy.

> **DISTILLERY**
>
> KENTUCKY
>
> **Owner:** Heaven Hill Distilleries
>
> **Established:** 1890
>
> **Status:** Destroyed in 1996, production continues in Louisville

Heaven Hill Old Style Bourbon. 40% ABV. Color: Straw gold.

Jack Daniel's

Jasper Newton Daniel, nicknamed "Jack," set up this legendary distillery in Lynchburg, Tennessee, when he was just 20 years old. The whiskey is trickled through ten feet of hard maple charcoal to give the distinctive Tennessee character. In 1890, he began producing No.7, with its distinctive black label and four-cornered bottle. In 1904, at the St. Louis World's Fair, it was proclaimed "the best whiskey in the world." It is now the best-selling whiskey in the USA.

Tasting Notes

The nose is fiery and full of energy, with notes of oak and licorice. It is heavy on the palate at first, then milder, very oily, with notes of caramel. The finish is very long with notes of corn and malt.

Jack Daniel's Old No.7.
40% ABV. Color: Copper red.

TENNESSEE	DISTILLERY
Owner: Brown-Forman	
Established: 1866	
Annual Production: Not specified	

Jim Beam

Jim Beam owns two distilleries that produce its standard brand, the second-best-selling whiskey after Jack Daniel's No.7. The original distillery is located in Clermont, south of Louisville; the second, built in 1953, is in Boston. The two distilleries use exactly the same methods but the water sources are different and, although the recipe is kept secret, it is likely that the whiskies are blended with each other to ensure consistency.

Tasting Notes

The nose has vanilla and delicate floral notes. The palate is initially sweet, with notes of vanilla, then drier, oaky notes develop. The finish is malty with a hint of vanilla.

Jim Beam Kentucky Straight Bourbon, 'White Label.' 40% ABV. Color: Straw gold.

KENTUCKY | DISTILLERY

Owner: Diageo

Established: ca.1870

Annual Production: 10,570,000 gallons

Kentucky Gentleman

The Barton Distillery is located in picturesque Bardstown, southwest of Louisville, although the distillery itself is somewhat less than picturesque, being a brick-built factory with the fermentation tanks located outside along with the isolation still. Huge warehouses are dotted around the expansive property. The company specializes in the production of very affordable and, for the most part, perfectly acceptable whiskies.

DISTILLERY

KENTUCKY

Owner: Constellation Brands

Established: 1890

Annual Production: Not specified

Kentucky Gentleman. 50% ABV. Color: Amber.

Tasting Notes

An exceptionally powerful whiskey; only a light aroma of malt comes through in the nose. The body is explosively sweet, with strong rye notes and a hint of caramel. The finish is long and dry with a hint of wood and vanilla.

Tasting Notes

The trademark wax seal is a sign of quality that is revealed immediately in the full nose with strong notes of vanilla and wood, and a hint of cloves. It is soft on the palate, with vanilla and caramel dominating. The finish is smooth, clean, and satisfyingly long.

Maker's Mark
Kentucky Straight
Bourbon, "Red Seal."
45% ABV.
Color: Dark gold.

DISTILLERY

KENTUCKY

Owner: Fortune Brands

Established: 1805

Annual Production: Not specified

Maker's Mark

Located four miles outside the town of Loretto, Kentucky, the Maker's Mark Distillery is a haven of traditional whisky production (here spelt without the "e"—a clue to the Scottish origins of the Samuels family who founded the distillery).

Production is supervised by the seventh consecutive generation of the family even though the firm is now owned by Fortune. Work is done exclusively by manual labor, explaining the modest daily output of 54 barrels.

Old Forester

Produced in Shively, Kentucky, Old Forester 86 Proof is made in the same time-honored style originated by George Garvin Brown in 1870: twice-distilled, using a mash high in rye and fermented for five days with a proprietary yeast strain. It is aged in charred oak barrels handcrafted at the distillery's own cooperage and is bottled when the Master Distiller judges the whiskey ready. In fact, George Brown was the first to sell his whiskey exclusively in glass bottles.

Tasting Notes

It has a well-balanced aroma of wood and fruit, with notes of vanilla and just a hint of cloves. The taste is a crisp and clean rye, with notes of fruit. The finish is long and smooth with hints of vanilla and caramel.

Old Forester Kentucky Straight Bourbon.
43% ABV.
Color: Rich amber.

KENTUCKY

DISTILLERY

Owner: Brown-Forman

Established: ca.1870

Annual Production: Not specified

Wild Turkey

The Kentucky River provides a charming setting for the Wild Turkey Distillery in the small town of Lawrenceburg, Kentucky. Formerly known as the Boulevard Distillery, it was founded by D.L. Moore in 1869 and sold to the Ripy brothers from Ireland in 1907. Although the exact mash recipe is a closely guarded secret, the bourbon is said to be as much as 75 percent corn, 13 percent rye, and 12 percent malted barley.

Tasting Notes

The nose is wonderfully floral with notes of honey and mild spice. It is at first rather strong on the palate, then becomes softer and drier with notes of honey and orange. The finish is long and nutty.

Wild Turkey Rare Breed Kentucky Straight Bourbon. 54.1% ABV. Color: Dark amber.

KENTUCKY   **DISTILLERY**

Owner: Pernod Ricard

Established: 1869

Annual Production: 2,850,000 gallons

Tasting Notes

The nose carries an intense aroma of vanilla with just a hint of fruit. On the palate it is very full, slightly spicy, and not very sweet. The finish is long and warming.

DISTILLERY

KENTUCKY

Owner: Brown-Forman

Established: 1812

Annual Production: Not specified

Woodford Reserve
Kentucky Straight
Bourbon.
45.2% ABV.
Color: Amber gold.

Woodford Reserve

The Woodford Reserve Distillery is located in Glenn's Creek, Versailles, Kentucky. It was founded by Elijah Pepper in 1812. However, it was Dr. James Crow, who joined the distillery after Elijah's death, who was responsible for perfecting the sour-mash method that led to the first production of true bourbon. Woodford Reserve bourbon is a blend of triple-distilled bourbon from the Woodford Distillery and straight bourbon from the Brown-Forman Distillery.

AROUND THE WORLD

Scotland, Ireland, the United States, and Canada are traditionally the big four whiskey-producing nations, but there are many other emergent whiskey powerhouses, not least Japan.

Japan began to distill its own whiskey in the early 20th century and today it has its own whiskey style, albeit firmly entrenched in the Scottish tradition, which is why "whisky" from Japan is spelt without the "e." It has a characteristically oily texture with a clean, malty flavor and very mild peatiness. Although it is still most popular in its home market, Japanese whisky is increasingly appreciated in the export market and it is now the fourth largest whiskey-producing nation—knocking Ireland into fifth place.

Canada has a proud whisky heritage dating back to the end of the 18th century in Ontario and Quebec, in the areas surrounding the

Great Lakes, which is where Canadian "whisky" (here also usually spelt without the "e") was first produced on a regular basis. Today, Canada is the world's third largest whiskey producer, with over 200 million bottles produced annually. However, there are just ten distilleries that continue to make typical Canadian whisky, in which rye whisky with its characteristic spiciness is blended with other grain whiskies.

Although it is currently better known for its beer and wine production, Australia has a great whisky tradition thanks to the influence of British colonial rule. Similarly, Indian whisky production dates back to the days of British colonialism. In recent years,

fed by the boom in the Indian economy, whiskey production has increased massively. It is worth noting that liberal laws in India permit a distillate made from molasses to be sold as "whisky," which in the West would be categorized as rum. Nevertheless, some excellent traditional whiskies are being produced, although they are difficult to obtain.

Whiskey is currently being distilled in more than twenty countries around the world. Although a few distilleries, such as Japan's Hakushu, are vast, the majority are small and experimental, using new techniques of production and maturation. Consequently, it is an exciting time for whiskey lovers who can expect to experience many new flavors.

Amrut

Radhakrishna Jagdale founded the company in 1948 and, today, Amrut—meaning "water of life" in Sanskrit—is India's largest distillery. The whisky is made from barley grown in the Punjab and Rajasthan provinces of India, with Himalayan water. The malting takes place in Jaipur and Delhi and the whisky is distilled in the "boomtown" of Bangalore, where it is aged for three years in bourbon and oak casks. Amrut Single Malt Whisky, made from unpeated malt, is now available worldwide.

Tasting Notes

The nose reveals a rather fruity and sweet malt note with notes of chocolate and spice. Robust on the palate, the flavor conveys this fruity sweetness as well as a hint of black coffee. A clear oak note is discernible in the finish.

BANGALORE	DISTILLERY
Owner: Jagdale Group	
Established: 1948	
Annual Production: 528,000 gallons	

Amrut Fusion Single Malt.
Aged 3 years. 50% ABV.
Color: Flaxen gold.

Bakery Hill

David Baker first started distilling in 2000, two years after he founded the business in Melbourne, Australia. This skilled food chemist manufactures Australian single malt in a small pot still, using the Scottish method with malts from both domestic and Scottish sources. The distillery offers five varieties of single malt, all of which are single-cask bottled. Bakery Hill has already received numerous awards and is generally considered to produce the finest whisky in Australia.

DISTILLERY

MELBOURNE

Owner: Dave Baker

Established: 1998

Annual Production: Not specified

Bakery Hill Single Malt (Cask Strength). 60% ABV. Color: Rich gold.

Tasting Notes

The aroma is very smoky, with a hint of salt and notes of lemon and cherry. The palate contains a hint of caramel, honey, and a strong malty note. The finish is long, warming, and well rounded, again with a wisp of smoke.

Black Velvet

The Black Velvet Distillery
stands on the eastern edge of
the Rocky Mountains in the
little town of Lethridge, Alberta,
Canada. Its blend is among
the best-selling whiskies in
Canada. Black Velvet first
came out of the barrel
in 1951. Started by
Gilbeys Gin, the brand
was initially known as
"Black Label," but after
Jack Napier, the original
distiller, sampled the
first batch he changed
the name to Black Velvet
to reflect its "uncommon
velvety taste."

DISTILLERY

ALBERTA

Owner: Schenley
Distilleries

Established: 1945

Annual Production:
Not specified

Black Velvet. Blended.
40% ABV.
Color: Rich gold.

Tasting Notes

A distinctly peppery note
emerges on the nose, with
notes of corn and rye. On
the palate it is slightly
sweet with toffee and
chocolate notes. The finish
is short and a little spicy.

Forty Creek

Founded in the 1970s by Otto Rieder, the Kittling Ridge Distillery is located in Grimsby, Ontario. John Hall bought the company in 1992 and began to distill his own whisky, Forty Creek, which takes its name from the little stream on which the distillery was built. The whisky is distilled in copper pot stills from a combination of corn, barley, and rye. It is stored in charred oak casks for early aging, with further maturation in sherry barrels.

Tasting Notes

The nose offers aromas of vanilla, toasted oak, and fruit. Vanilla appears anew on the palate, with notes of walnut, honey, and spices. Vanilla surfaces again in the smooth finish.

Forty Creek 'Barrel Select'. Blended. 40% ABV. Color: Amber.

ONTARIO

DISTILLERY

Owner: John K. Hall

Established: 1992

Annual Production: Not specified

Potter's Special Old

CANADA

In Kelowna, in the beautiful Okanagan Valley, lies the Potter Disillery. Ernie Potter founded the distillery in 1958. It originally only bottled and sold liqueurs but, over the years, expanded into spirits. In 2005, the distillery was bought by Highwood Distillers. This independent company wanted to expand its portfolio and sought a new facility since its own production capacity was about to be reached.

Tasting Notes

The aroma presents a clear rye note, typical of Canadian whisky. The palate offers light caramel with walnut and rye. Vanilla and oak appear in the medium-long finish.

Potter's Special Old. Aged 14 years. 40% ABV. Color: Pale amber.

ALBERTA	DISTILLERY
Owner: Highwood Distillers Ltd	
Established: 1958	
Annual Production: 1,320,000 gallons	

Tasting Notes

The nose is buttery with notes of caramel. The flavor is fruity with notes of peat. The finish is dry with a touch of leather.

GoldCock Single Malt.
Aged 12 years.
43% ABV.
Color: Pale gold.

GoldCock

The Jelinek Distillery is located in the town of Vizovice in the Czech Republic. After decades of state ownership under the socialist government, the business was privatized in 1989. It uses Moravian barley malt in a copper pot still to produce whisky with a delicate flavor that typically has a peat-smoke aroma and notes of wood from the oak casks used for maturation.

DISTILLERY

VIZOVICE

Owner: R. Jelinek

Established: 1894

Annual Production: Not specified

Tasting Notes

The aroma is fruity with notes of butter and smoke. On the palate, the butter is complemented by chocolate and notes of raisins and dried figs against a background of oak. The finish is slightly bitter at first and brings out the mild notes of smoke toward the end.

DISTILLERY

NORTH OF STOCKHOLM

Owner: Mackmyra Svensk Whisky

Established: 1999

Annual Production: Not specified

Mackmyra Preludium 03 Single Malt.
52.2% ABV.
Color: Golden yellow.

Mackmyra Preludium

A group of single-malt enthusiasts funded the distillery sited in Valbo, Sweden. The company began by experimenting with a small, self-built still that had a capacity of no more than 100 litres. New facilities were installed in 2002, and the first Mackmyra Preludium Single Malt was sold in 2006. The smoky Preludium 03 Single Malt is matured in bourbon casks and finished in sherry casks.

Hakushu

The Hakushu Distillery, situated to the west of Tokyo in the foothills of the Japanese Alps, is the world's largest whisky-producing facility. With 24 column stills, close to seven million gallons of spirits can be produced here annually. Approximately 800,000 barrels are stored in the numerous warehouses. Naturally, most of the whisky is used for blends. However, Hakushu single malts are considered to be the Japanese whisky of choice.

DISTILLERY

FUJI GOTEMBA

Owner: Suntory

Established: 1973

Annual Production:
6,870,000 gallons

The Hakushu
Single Malt Whisky.
Aged 18 years.
43% ABV.
Color: Amber.

Tasting Notes

The aroma is citrusy with a note of barley. The barley is developed on the palate, with a malty sweetness. The medium-long finish reveals light traces of chocolate and vanilla.

Nikka Sendai

The Sendai Distillery lies in the Hirose Valley on the outskirts of Sendai in Japan's Miyagi Prefecture. The red-brick building was constructed in 1969 along Scottish lines, right down to the characteristic pagoda roof. From the beginning, there were two distilleries: Miyagikyo is the second and slightly lesser known Nikka distillery. Most of the whisky produced here goes into Nikka's range of blended whisky, but a small amount is produced as a single malt under the Miyagikyo name.

Nikka Miyagikyo Single Malt. Aged 15 years. 45% ABV. Color: Amber.

Tasting Notes

The rich aroma has dried fruit and sherry notes, with hints of earthy peat and smoke. It is slightly oily on the palate, with some honey and dried fruits and spices. Dried fruits return in the medium-long finish, with a touch of wood.

DISTILLERY

NIKKA MIYAGIKYO

Owner: Nikka

Established: 1969

Annual Production: 1,320,000 gallons

Tasting Notes

The nose is very pleasing with aromas of honey and dried fruits. On the palate it is slightly spicy, but with a very pleasant feel in the mouth. The finish has a nicely dry, lingering woody note.

DISTILLERY

OSAKA

Owner: Suntory

Established: 1923

Annual Production: 920,000 gallons

The Yamazaki Single Malt. Aged 12 years. 43% ABV. Color: Pale amber.

Yamazaki

As proudly stated on the label, Yamazaki is Japan's oldest distillery, founded in 1923 by Shinjiro Torii with the help of Masataka Taketsuru, who had learned his trade in Scotland. The first Yamazaki whisky was released on the market six years after the distillery was built. The original 14 pot stills were replaced in the 1990s with a multiplicity of stills in various shapes and sizes, which enabled the firm to produce a more varied selection of whiskies.

Picture Credits

The publisher would like to thank the distilleries and agencies who supplied all of the images in this book.

AB InBev p. 27.

BC Partners p. 39.

Beam Inc. p. 34, 36.

Brown-Forman p. 45, 49, 51.

Constellation Brands p. 47.

Dave Baker p. 5, 55.

Diageo p. 1, 11, 12, 13, 17, 19, 22, 23, 24, 25, 29, 33, 46.

Dickel p. 42.

Edrington Group p. 16.

Fortune Brands p. 7, 20, 48.

Heaven Hill Distilleries p. 44.

Highwood Distillers Ltd p. 58.

Inver House p. 8.

J&A Mitchell p. 28.

Jagdale Group p.54.

John K. Hall p. 57.

Kirin p. 43.

Loch Lomond Distillers p. 2, 21.

Mackmyra Svensk Whisky p. 60.

Nikka p. 62.

Pernod Ricard p. 14, 26, 30, 35, 37, 38, 50.

Picard Vins & Spiritueux p. 31.

R. Jelinek p. 59.

Sazerac p. 41.

Schenley Distilleries p. 56.

Suntory p. 61, 63.

United Breweries Group p.10.

United Spirits Group p. 18;

William Grant & Sons p. 9, 15.